ULTIMATE C

Contents

LEADER'S GUIDE

These guidelines will help you get the most out of the studies.

1. Set out in advance the dates, time, and place of all the studies, and make sure everyone is aware of them. It is usually best to keep these the same each week.

2. Each person should have a copy of this book and be able to see a Bible.

3. Before each meeting, the leader of that session should:

   a) read the Bible passage carefully, referring to a Bible dictionary or commentary if necessary.

   b) read the comment on the passage and think about how to use this information in the discussion, then look at any other Bible passages suggested and consider if they should be brought into the discussion.

   c) think about the questions. Some groups may want to talk about them all, some groups may not. Use those most appropriate to your group.

4. At the meeting:

   a) read the Bible passages aloud. Get one or two people to do this but remember that not everyone enjoys reading aloud and some may be embarrassed if they feel they cannot do it well.

   b) you may wish to begin by mentioning some of the key points in the comment or start with the questions. Encourage people to relate the discussion both to the text and to real-life situations.

   c) try to make sure that everyone who wants to speak has an opportunity to do so. Summarize the conclusions of a discussion at the end.

   d) spend some time praying together. Use the suggested prayers, but feel free to develop your own which arise from the discussion. Encourage people to pray briefly and simply. Be sensitive to some people's hesitations and difficulties about praying aloud.

   e) decide who is going to lead the next session and ask the group to read the passage and comment before the meeting.

   f) if any group members are absent from a session, contact them the following day and let them know they were missed. Check that they know the arrangements for the next meeting.

INTRODUCTION

In all six parables set for study in this book Jesus presents people with stark alternatives and choices. These parables do not sit comfortably with a detached interest in Christian life and discipleship. There is no place here for the uncommitted. Casual observation at a distance is not the mood to bring to these passages of Scripture.

I once sat high up on a hill looking down on two walkers coming to a fork in the path. I could see clearly from my vantage point that one path led nowhere — it petered out among gorse and thickets. The other path was clearly the one they needed to choose. I was too far away to offer advice. I could only look on as an observer of their ordeal as, for what seemed several minutes, they wrestled over which option to choose. I felt for them but in the end it did not make any difference to me. I was an observer of the drama. The Christian is not as I was then, a casual observer. The follower of Christ is always the person at the crossroads.

The parables are often about the Kingdom of God; God's reign and rule in people's lives, in communities and in the world. It is because God's reign is absolute that we are not allowed the luxury of standing on the sideline, of being spectators and armchair observers in the issues which are at stake. We *must* choose. It is because his reign is comprehensive that we cannot be selective about the areas where we do or do not yield to his rule and live by the values of his Kingdom. We must make choices in *all* areas of life.

These are ultimate choices — choices about fundamental attitudes, values and goals in your life. These are moments of crisis. Everything hangs on the path you choose, the decision you make, the option you embrace.

Many Christians coast along, free-wheeling their way through life, allowing themselves to be carried along by whatever influences and pressures are around them at the time. They are like thermometers, simply reflecting the prevailing climate. But as disciples of Christ we are called positively to influence the climate around, like thermostats. That means taking a grip of life and in the face of daily options, in both large and small matters, choosing what is right and pleasing to God.

If this sounds like a heavy responsibility to bear, then remember you are never asked to make a choice without light being shed on the dilemma. You are not asked to leap in the dark. One path is the illuminated way, the other is unilluminated. The parables are told in order to nudge people in the right direction. You may be at the crossroads, but you are not without a map and compass. The clear guidance of Jesus' teaching is there to steer you into the right path.

The theme of these studies is one that Christians need to heed. They often have to face moments of crisis — decisive moments — where the credibility of their Christian discipleship depends on the courage and determination to make right choices rather than remain comfortably detached.

The parables are often followed by questions from Jesus, pressing his hearers to make choices, and those questions come loud and clear to us as we study these passages: "What do you think. . .?" "Which of these two . . .?" Because these parables call for a response it would be helpful if in studying them within a group there could be some covenant of action, an agreement that you will be "doers of the Word and not hearers only" (James 1.22, AV).

THE TWO HOUSE BUILDERS

AIM

To understand the choices we make about building our lives on the teaching of Jesus.

MATTHEW 7.24-29

[24]"So then, anyone who hears these words of mine and obeys them is like a wise man who built his house on rock. [25]The rain poured down, the rivers overflowed, and the wind blew hard against that house. But it did not fall, because it was built on rock.

[26]"But anyone who hears these words of mine and does not obey them is like a foolish man who built his house on sand. [27]The rain poured down, the rivers overflowed, the wind blew hard against that house, and it fell. And what a terrible fall that was!"

[28]When Jesus finished saying these things, the crowd was amazed at the way he taught. [29]He wasn't like the teachers of the Law; instead, he taught with authority.

It is fitting that at the beginning of our study of these New Testament parables we consider the choices we must repeatedly make about how we respond to Jesus' teaching. After all, this parable of the two house builders deals with how we might respond to the other five parables in this book.

The scene described here was familiar enough. During the summer months in Palestine many dry and sandy water channels (called wadis) would appear to foolish people attractive sites to build houses, without the hassle of having to dig foundations in rocky ground. But when the rainy season came those houses in the wadis stood no chance against the might of rain, flood and wind. Houses on which more time and effort had been spent, with their foundations firmly secured in the rock, would withstand the onslaught and remain upright.

By way of application Jesus presents a stark alternative. You may choose to build your life on the foundation of practical obedience to Jesus' teaching, or you may choose wilfully to resist his authority (verse 29). The way the sentence is constructed in verse 27 emphasizes the gravity of the situation.

The words "so then" in verse 24 alert us to the sayings which have gone before and which are now going to be driven home in specific application. True as against false discipleship is a key theme in what we know as the Sermon on the Mount (Matthew chapters 5-7). Immediately prior to this parable of the two houses (verses 21-23) Jesus has plainly stated that obedience to him is a sure sign of the reality of a person's discipleship.

Every day things happen to us and situations arise to which we must react as Christians. What does the Lord want me to do in the face of this situation? For example, someone at work misunderstands me or taunts me about my Christian faith. How do I react to that situation? What would be a reaction shaped by the teaching of Jesus? (Matthew 5.12 may help.) Or I may fall ill, or be provoked to impatience by the behaviour of my child, or be made redundant.

But Christians ought not simply to wait for things to happen to them before seeking out the will and purpose of the Lord. We ought to look first at the teaching and then positively and deliberately put that teaching into practice. For example, in many areas of life, by the way we relate to other people, by the values we embrace and the lifestyle we adopt we could influence the world for good (Matthew 5.16 may help).

So whether reacting to situations or taking the initiative, our choices should be shaped by the teaching of Jesus and the values of his Kingdom. In Matthew chapters 5-7 many aspects of that Kingdom teaching are gathered together. We either hear his voice and allow the gentle but insistent pressure of his word to result in action pleasing to him and in keeping with his values or we resist that pressure and wilfully go our own way.

IDENTIFYING WITH THE STORY

Recall some course of action you have taken or some choice you have made which turned out to be mistaken and perhaps disastrous. How did you feel at the time, and what were the consequences of your mistake for yourself and others?

QUESTIONS AND ACTIVITIES

1. Why should Jesus carry more authority in your life than other people?

2. Share within the group some situations in which you have had to make choices about how you reacted. For example, somebody pushes

in front of you in the supermarket queue — how do you react? Sometimes we have to respond almost immediately, without much time for thought; consider how the teaching of Jesus helps to guide your reaction, especially when time is short.

3. Why is it easier to hear the teaching of Jesus and then ignore or resist it rather than obey it?

4. In the daily choices which must be made, what practical help would it be to ask the question: "What is the short-term gain of choosing this option against the long-term implications of choosing another?" You may think of some examples, such as whether or not you watch a particular TV programme, or whether or not you visit someone.

5. What elements of a typical service in your church help you to be obedient to God's word, rather than just make you feel good?

PRAYER SUGGESTIONS

Members of the group may feel able to recite or read out a saying of Jesus which expresses his will.

Beginning each time with "Jesus said", such commands as the following could be used:

"Whoever remains in me . . . will bear much fruit." (John 15.5)

". . . don't be all upset, always concerned about what you will eat and drink . . . Instead, be concerned with his Kingdom . . ." (Luke 12.29,31)

After each statement, pause so that the word of the Lord may be received and accepted and a quiet commitment made to do what the Lord says.

Acknowledge that in many ways and at many times we have failed to obey the commands of Jesus.

Give thanks for the breadth of Jesus' teaching and its relevance for today.

Pray for Christians who in some countries of the world are facing persecution and suffering because of their commitment to Christ.

OTHER PASSAGES

Deuteronomy 28
Psalm 119.9-16
James 1.22-27
John 15.9-17

1 cor 3 v 11-15

THE PHARISEE AND THE TAX COLLECTOR

AIM _____

To understand the choices we make about seeking a right relationship with God.

LUKE 18.9-14

⁹Jesus also told this parable to people who were sure of their own goodness and despised everybody else. ¹⁰"Once there were two men who went up to the Temple to pray: one was a Pharisee, the other a tax collector.

¹¹"The Pharisee stood apart by himself and prayed, 'I thank you, God, that I am not greedy, dishonest, or an adulterer, like everybody else. I thank you that I am not like that tax collector over there. ¹²I fast two days a week, and I give you a tenth of all my income.'

¹³"But the tax collector stood at a distance and would not even raise his face to heaven, but beat on his breast and said, 'God, have pity on me, a sinner!' ¹⁴I tell you," said Jesus, "the tax collector, and not the Pharisee, was in the right with God when he went home. For everyone who makes himself great will be humbled, and everyone who humbles himself will be made great."

Before we start thinking about living the Christian life we must be clear about how we enter into a right relationship with God. This parable deals with the important choice facing all who seek to be right with God.

You might choose the way of the Pharisee. At first glance it looks an attractive way. It certainly fits in with the thinking of our day which applauds self-effort and personal initiative. The famous Frank Sinatra song "I did it my way" sounds praiseworthy and suggests enterprise. And the Pharisee in this parable was likewise a self-made man who relished his achievements and his moral respectability. But for someone wanting to be right with God, the Pharisee had chosen a path with a dead end.

He found himself on the wrong path not least because he made a wrong comparison. He compared himself with other people rather than with God (verse 11). We will all find it easy to think of people with whom we compare favourably in terms of, for example, honesty, kindness, faithfulness, loyalty. We make these comparisons constantly as individuals and delight in chalking up points when we think we score over others, saying with the Pharisee: "I am grateful I am not like that person . . .". And probably we are right some of the time. The Pharisee certainly was very virtuous, and the tax collector was no saint.

But when you resist the Pharisee's way and measure yourself against the purity, holiness, truth and beauty of God, you immediately see how far short you come of meeting his standards. When the character of Jesus Christ is the benchmark by which you evaluate your character, you see how morally bankrupt and poverty-stricken you really are.

It is then that the tax collector's way of approach is appreciated as the only means of entering into a right relationship with God. At the heart of his prayer in the temple was an understanding of what the Bible means by "grace". You do not have to understand fully the deep riches of this term to experience what it means, namely that God comes to meet you with undeserved and unmerited love and mercy, holding out to you forgiveness and a way into his family without your having to earn it.

Easy as this may sound, in practice it runs contrary to our instinct, which finds receiving salvation as a free gift difficult. The Holy Spirit alone can enable us honestly and sincerely to say with the Psalmist, "I have sinned . . . have mercy on me" (Psalm 41.4). But the question is, are you willing to let go of self-righteousness and be helped to make that confession?

You cannot face a more important choice than the way you respond to God's offer of free grace through Jesus Christ. You can by faith receive God's promise and accept his gift or, like the Pharisee, maintain the illusion that by your own merit and effort, by trusting in yourself, you can earn the right to a place in God's friendship and family.

IDENTIFYING WITH THE STORY

In what areas of life and on what issues do you compare yourself favourably or unfavourably with other people? What do you learn about yourself, your values, the things that really matter to you? Come on now, be absolutely honest with yourself and with each other.

QUESTIONS AND ACTIVITIES

1. Look at Luke's account of the woman who poured perfume over Jesus' feet (Luke 7.36-50). How do you show in your life, either as an

9

individual or with others, your thankfulness to God for his goodness and free gift of grace?

2. Many Christians are concerned about their inability to put their faith into practice in their daily lives. How should the way we behave relate to our beliefs?

3. Someone gives you a present. You feel indebted. You either want to pay for it or look for some opportunity to return the generosity — put the score even again. Why is this? Why do we usually find it more difficult to receive from other people than to give? Jesus explains that the issue at stake is whether or not a person is prepared to be humble. What do you understand by humility? What is it that is humbling about receiving both God's free gift of mercy and his forgiveness?

4. How would you answer someone who honestly says that they have lived a good and decent life and will go to heaven?

5. How do you feel about the fact that God's gift of salvation takes away the responsibility of struggling and striving to earn your own salvation?

PRAYER SUGGESTIONS

Share with each other patterns of daily worship and devotion which have helped you keep fresh your sense of gratitude to God and your desire to live to his glory.

Let two or three lead the group in confessing the stubbornness with which we cling to the illusion that by our own efforts we can establish and maintain a right relationship with God.

Through various means — a line or two of a song or hymn, a verse of Scripture, a sentence prayer — let the group express its praise for God's grace (his undeserved love and mercy) revealed supremely in the life, death, resurrection and abiding presence of Jesus.

OTHER PASSAGES

Psalm 51.1-12
Luke 7.36-50
Acts 15.5-11
Romans 3.21-28

THE TWO SONS

AIM

To understand the choices we make about responding to God's call.

MATTHEW 21.28-32

[28]"Now, what do you think? There was once a man who had two sons. He went to the elder one and said, 'Son, go and work in the vineyard today.' [29]'I don't want to,' he answered, but later he changed his mind and went. [30]Then the father went to the other son and said the same thing. 'Yes, sir,' he answered, but he did not go. [31]Which one of the two did what his father wanted?"

"The elder one," they answered.

So Jesus said to them, "I tell you: the tax collectors and the prostitutes are going into the Kingdom of God ahead of you. [32]For John the Baptist came to you showing you the right path to take, and you would not believe him; but the tax collectors and the prostitutes believed him. Even when you saw this, you did not later change your minds and believe him."

This parable stands apart from the others we are considering for this reason: there is no straight choice to make between the right and the wrong path. The truth is that both sons in the story came short of the ideal. Again the raw material of the story is very down to earth and we will readily recognize ourselves and others, for we have surely all behaved in this way.

On being asked by his father to undertake work in the vineyard the elder son is awkward, his initial response is hard and surly. But in the event he changes his mind and responds positively to his father's request. The second son quickly says yes and seems to promise a great deal. But in the event he does not keep his word.

True as it is that neither son represents the ideal, when it comes to our relationship with God there is a choice to make. Jesus implies as much by the question he poses (verse 31), "Which one of the two did what his father wanted?" Clearly not the second son. To bring to God an initial enthusiasm and willing spirit counts for nothing if it evaporates almost as soon as the word is spoken and the promise made.

But the parable holds out hope to those who initially resist the good news of God but in the end repent and become steadfast and faithful servants of the one whose word they at first rejected. The Gentiles (verse 43) were to inherit the privileges once given to the Jewish people.

In the mind of Jesus the tax collectors and the outcasts were represented by the elder son. At first glance they look unlikely materials for Jesus to use in building his Kingdom. The religious people, the outwardly pious, look much more promising and the second son, at first eager and willing, represents them.

The parable illustrates the danger of a cheap and enthusiastic profession of faith which is proved unreal by a life not matching the profession. Several factors can lull us into this condition. Two which are particularly around today are an emphasis on the *emotional* side of Christian faith — on feelings and subjective experience — and *familiarity* with the things of God. The more enthusiastic and vibrant our worship, the more carefully should we examine the words we sing and say, ensuring that what we offer in praise on a Sunday morning is worked out in practice on a Monday morning. For example, to sing "Here I am, wholly available, as for me I will serve the Lord" commits you to a life of single-minded devotion to the will and glory of God, whether that be at an office desk, at a factory bench or as a missionary. It is a perilous thing to make such a promise to God and then not fulfil it.

But the parable also holds out the opportunity of starting again, following true repentance. The son who at first resisted his father's request but then changed his mind (repented) is an encouraging illustration that failure need never be final. Here is hope for those who think they are hopeless and who reckon that they have had their chance and blown it. In Jesus' day there were many who were at the margins of respectable society and beyond the scope of organized religion. But these were among the first to respond to the good news that God's Kingdom was open to tax collectors, outcasts and prostitutes.

IDENTIFYING WITH THE STORY

Think of occasions recently when you promised with zeal to do something (maybe play with the children or write a letter) and in the event you did not. Or recall times when in haste you rejected a request but then later wished you had not. How do you feel about your responses on those occasions and what do you learn from them about human nature?

QUESTIONS AND ACTIVITIES

1. How can you keep alive over weeks, months and years your initial enthusiasm for Christian discipleship? How do you know when this enthusiasm is fading? What are the danger signs?

2. How do you feel when someone breaks a promise or lets you down? How easy do you find it to forgive them and renew your trust? Think about these things in the light of God's constant desire to forgive and search after those who reject him.

3. In the parable the elder son found it possible to have a change of heart which brought him into line with his father's wishes. How does this make you feel? What is your response?

4. Look at Isaiah 29.13 and compare with Matthew 15.7-9. What effect is there on a watching world when Christians say a great deal but then seem not to carry into practice what they preach?

5. Is there anyone in the group able to share a story of someone who seemed to be beyond the reach of the gospel but who is now a Christian?

PRAYER SUGGESTIONS

Let one or two members of the group offer prayers of confession that on many occasions we have made promises to God and to other people which we have failed to keep. Admit that because of this we have brought disappointment and sadness to those we let down.

Pray for Christians working in situations where there appears to be constant resistance to the appeal of the gospel. Pray that the people of God there may be encouraged by the truth of this passage, that the most unfruitful ground can ultimately bear a good harvest.

Pray too for those who once turned their backs on the gospel and believe now that there is no way for them to change their minds.

OTHER PASSAGES

Job 1.1-3, 3.1-5
Matthew 26.31-35, 56(b), 69-75
Luke 15.11-32

THE GOOD SAMARITAN

AIM

To understand the choices we make in the face of human need.

LUKE 10.25-37

[25]A teacher of the Law came up and tried to trap Jesus. "Teacher," he asked, "what must I do to receive eternal life?"

[26]Jesus answered him, "What do the Scriptures say? How do you interpret them?"

[27]The man answered, "'Love the Lord your God with all your heart, with all your soul, with all your strength, and with all your mind'; and 'Love your neighbour as you love yourself.'"

[28]"You are right," Jesus replied; "do this and you will live."

[29]But the teacher of the Law wanted to justify himself, so he asked Jesus, "Who is my neighbour?"

[30]Jesus answered, "There was once a man who was going down from Jerusalem to Jericho when robbers attacked him, stripped him, and beat him up, leaving him half dead. [31]It so happened that a priest was going down that road: but when he saw the man, he walked on by, on the other side. [32]In the same way a Levite also came along, went over and looked at the man, and then walked on by, on the other side. [33]But a Samaritan who was travelling that way came upon the man, and when he saw him, his heart was filled with pity. [34]He went over to him, poured oil and wine on his wounds and bandaged them; then he put the man on his own animal and took him to an inn, where he took care of him. [35]The next day he took out two silver coins and gave them to the innkeeper. 'Take care of him,' he told the innkeeper, 'and when I come back this way, I will pay you whatever else you spend on him.'"

[36]And Jesus concluded, "In your opinion, which one of these three acted like a neighbour towards the man attacked by the robbers?"

[37]The teacher of the Law answered, "The one who was kind to him." Jesus replied, "You go, then, and do the same."

A desert road, twisty, lined with many rocks and caves and which drops some 3,600 feet in almost twenty miles is bound to attract muggers. The scene which Jesus dramatically describes was familiar enough to his audience.

Note the setting. The parable is told in response to some questions from an expert in the Jewish law. The strong impression comes across that here is someone very glad to discuss abstract matters and thorny problems. His aim is to score points in this debate with Jesus, to "justify himself". There is also a hint in this man's questioning that he wants to know how near to himself he can draw the boundary line of compassion.

But Jesus is having none of it. In response to his delight in abstract debate Jesus concentrates this Jewish leader's mind on one particular person who becomes the victim of bandits on that notorious Jericho road. This Jewish theologian is firmly led from a debate about definitions to a story about relationships.

In our day, when television brings into our homes graphic images of vast need in the world, it is all too easy for us to speak of "the problem of hunger", "the problem of divorce", "the problem of AIDS", etc. The size of these "problems" may so daunt us that we feel impotent to do any-thing about them, and that takes the edge off responsibility. In our own way we too can avoid the challenge of particular situations. By the flick of a switch we can turn off the television and push the "problem" away.

In applying this parable to ourselves, none of us can be neatly pigeon-holed as the priest, the Levite or the Samaritan. Truth to tell, there is a bit of each in all of us.

But this we can say: daily and often several times a day we will have to choose how we respond to Good Samaritan opportunities. These will reveal whether our religion is locked away in fine truth and high-sound-ing profession or is open to action and glad self-giving. And such oppor-tunities will come not only in dramatic ways with room for expansive gestures of self-sacrifice, but in many undramatic situations, requiring simple acts of courtesy, kindness and thoughtfulness.

Note that genuine love, flowing out from the life of God within, is an expression of the gospel and not merely a bait to draw people to Christ. Such love does not, therefore, have boundaries around it. Some argue that in Jesus' story the traveller was foolish to travel the Jericho road on his own and that, in a sense, he had only himself to blame. If God's love for us had had conditions about it, we would doubtless all have been excluded. It was in our folly and alienation that God loved us in Jesus Christ. So the love that we hold out to others must be equally free of con-ditions. We love as God has loved us.

The spirit of the priest and Levite is not far beneath the surface in all dis-ciples of Jesus Christ. These men were religious experts, but when the chips were down they failed in action pleasing to their God and in keep-ing with his word.

It is too easy for us, who are supposedly rich in the currency of love, to be conspicuous by our meanness when the need for love is greatest. And none of us is beyond inventing reasons for our inaction, equally as plausible as probably the priest and Levite could have offered. For example, one of the most subtle ways for Christians to avoid evangelism and costly service in the community is that we are so busy with church meetings and conferences. Often at these gatherings we earnestly discuss the importance of Christians' being released into other areas of responsible Christian involvement. But to discuss a thing is easier than to practise it. The truth is that sometimes we choose to pass by whilst non-Christians demonstrate the compassion which we profess.

The crisis for many Christians is whether we let perhaps legitimate but lesser claims on time and energy divert us from the primary claim on our lives to love God and for his sake to love those whom he allows to cross our paths. The question at the end (verse 36) focuses the choice which we must make. The legal expert was put on the spot, for in practice Jews believed that they were to be neighbours only to their own people. But Jesus gives the man no option but to admit that those who have the "eternal life" of God within them show the fact by a love which is costly in all its breadth and depth and length.

IDENTIFYING WITH THE STORY

Recall times when you came across someone who was hurt or in some kind of trouble. How did you react? How do you feel now about the way you reacted? Recall times when you felt uncared for, isolated, lonely and afraid. What did you long for at that time from other human beings?

QUESTIONS AND ACTIVITIES

1. What do you consider it means in popular thought today to be a neighbour? How do these ideas differ from and coincide with a Christian understanding of the term?

2. What devices do we use to turn blind eyes to the need around us? As a group go in imagination on a tour of your town and neighbourhood. Make a list of glaring needs which you see. Cheat a little and imagine that on your tour you have access to homes and institutions. In what ways does your church either encourage or discourage its members' being on the front line in responding with active love to those needs?

3. This expert in the Jewish law might have turned to any number of Old Testament scriptures which declared the will of God on these matters. Look, for example, at Leviticus 19.33-34. What practical ways are available to you for displaying the love of God to people in this country from all cultures and races?

4. How can individuals or a local church be kept alert to neglected opportunities for compassionate witness and service? In what ways could a church social responsibility committee or group help to fulfil this ministry to the church?

5. The parable challenges Christians about matters of justice. What local issues which reflect injustice and dishonour God's name should your church be responding to?

6. In what areas of life are you and other Christians not involved because of your church commitments?

PRAYER SUGGESTIONS

Acknowledge with gratitude that God's love has been poured into your heart through the Holy Spirit. Give thanks for occasions when in the Spirit's power that love has been revealed in your compassionate service.

Come clean with God that on many occasions you have turned a blind eye to need and "passed by on the other side". Receive afresh his forgiveness and yield again to the power of the Holy Spirit to amend what you are and direct what you will be in coming days.

Pray for those in your community who are either known to you or are as yet hidden from your view, whom God wants to reach out to through you. In praying for them commit yourself also to practical action.

Pray also for your church community, that together you may know great wisdom in the stewardship of members' time, energy and gifts.

OTHER PASSAGES

Amos 5.21-24
Matthew 25.31-45
1 John 4.7-21

HIDDEN TREASURE AND THE PEARL

AIM

To understand the choices we make about what we will value most highly in life.

> ### MATTHEW 13.44-46
>
> [44]"The Kingdom of heaven is like this. A man happens to find a treasure hidden in a field. He covers it up again, and is so happy that he goes and sells everything he has, and then goes back and buys that field.
>
> [45]"Also, the Kingdom of heaven is like this. A man is looking for fine pearls, [46]and when he finds one that is unusually fine, he goes and sells everything he has and buys that pearl."

There is a paradox at the heart of the gospel which faith grasps and understands but which faithless minds cannot see. For example, the gospel says that in giving up your freedom you discover real liberty, the liberty of being empowered to do God's will; in dying to self you discover what your life is really for; in abandoning an obsession with accumulating wealth, you discover the wealth which is found in a life given to joyful service and self-sacrifice. David Livingstone, reflecting on his experience as a missionary in Africa, said:

> For my own part, I have never ceased to rejoice that God has appointed me to such an office. People talk of the sacrifice I have made in spending so much of my life in Africa. Can that be called a sacrifice which is simply paid back as a small part of a great debt owing to our God, which we can never repay? Is that a sacrifice which brings its own blest reward in healthful activity, the consciousness of doing good, peace of mind, and a bright hope of a glorious destiny hereafter? Away with the word in such a view, and with such a thought! It is emphatically no sacrifice. Say rather it is a privilege… I never made a sacrifice. Of this we ought not to talk, when we remember the great sacrifice which he made who left his Father's throne on high to give himself for us.

Many are kept from entering into the "wealth" of God's Kingdom and family just because they are unwilling to surrender the "wealth" they have already accumulated: maybe material wealth, the wealth of status and power, the wealth of popularity, the wealth of independence and the right to control their own lives, the wealth of pride in what they are and what they have achieved. Many, when it comes to it, will choose not to give up trusting in all this rather than enter the Kingdom of God. Often it means surrendering not the inherently evil but the second best in order to possess the best (compare Mark 8.34-38). *Read*

That crisis moment of choice and decision certainly comes when, either suddenly or after a long search, we are first alerted to the appeal of the gospel. It is a critical moment for it may, but it may well not, come again.

But it is also true that in modern Western society, where values other than those of the Kingdom of God by and large rule the day and shape our lives, Christians must daily choose either to embrace the world's values or abandon them in order to live by the values of the Kingdom. Christians are kept at full stretch, each day making choices about priorities and what really matters most in life and to whose reign and rule they submit.

Placed alongside each other, these two parables helpfully parallel the different ways in which people discover the treasure of the gospel. The first man stumbled across the treasure, whilst the second man was actively searching for pearls. And Christian testimony illustrates both.

Some seem to stumble across the good news, and it takes them by surprise after maybe years of treading it underfoot. The dramatic awakening of people, from Saul on the Damascus Road to a prisoner I recently heard of, who came suddenly to faith through the witness and kindness of a prison visitor, illustrates that this is how the good news is discovered by some.

Others search for something to fill the empty space at the core of their being, and maybe only after a long journey God opens their eyes to the life which is in Christ.

There is room for both ways, and we must never imagine that there is a standard path for discovering the riches of the gospel. But however you come, that initial choice must still be made.

IDENTIFYING WITH THE STORY

Many examples spring to mind of people who have sacrificed something in order to make possible a greater good. You may have your own recollections of times when, in large or small ways, you have given up one thing in order to lay hold of something better. How did you come to those decisions and how did you feel about the sacrifices you were making, especially the risks that were entailed?

QUESTIONS AND ACTIVITIES

1. How does living for Christ affect your lifestyle in practical terms? What risks do you have to take? How vulnerable does this make you?

2. What happens if people only hear preaching that tells them their needs are met, rather than calling them to a costly adventure?

3. Let some within the group who are willing share the ways in which they came to personal faith. The variety of stories will be mutually encouraging and will generate thankfulness that in different ways God makes his grace available to people.

4. How can your church make all that God has to offer attractive to those outside the Church? What aspects of your church's life do that best?

5. How would you answer the person who accused Christianity of always asking its followers to give up the things they enjoy and find satisfying?

PRAYER SUGGESTIONS last

Give thanks for the measure to which your eyes have been opened by God's grace to see the surpassing wealth of being his children.

Lay honestly before God those occasions when you have settled for the safety of second-best "treasure", rather than taking risks and living adventurously for Christ.

Pray that your own lifestyle and that of other Christians and churches may be an increasingly powerful and attractive testimony.

OTHER PASSAGES

Mark 8.34-38
Luke 18.18-30
Luke 14.7-24
Philippians 3.7-8

THE TEN GIRLS

AIM

To understand the choices we make about preparing ourselves for future testing.

MATTHEW 25.1-13

[1]"At that time the Kingdom of heaven will be like this. Once there were ten girls who took their oil lamps and went out to meet the bridegroom. [2]Five of them were foolish, and the other five were wise. [3]The foolish ones took their lamps but did not take any extra oil with them, [4]while the wise ones took containers full of oil for their lamps. [5]The bridegroom was late in coming, so the girls began to nod and fall asleep.

[6]"It was already midnight when the cry rang out, 'Here is the bridegroom! Come and meet him!' [7]The ten girls woke up and trimmed their lamps. [8]Then the foolish ones said to the wise ones, 'Let us have some of your oil, because our lamps are going out.' [9]'No, indeed,' the wise ones answered, 'there is not enough for you and for us. Go to the shop and buy some for yourselves.' [10]So the foolish girls went off to buy some oil; and while they were gone, the bridegroom arrived. The five girls who were ready went in with him to the wedding feast, and the door was closed.

[11]"Later the other girls arrived. 'Sir, sir! Let us in!' they cried out. [12]'Certainly not! I don't know you,' the bridegroom answered."

[13]And Jesus concluded, "Be on your guard, then, because you do not know the day or the hour."

A Jewish marriage in Jesus' time involved a series of steps. The engagement (sometimes in childhood) was followed by the betrothal (just before marriageable age), and a year later came the wedding itself. This parable concerns the end of the process: the bridegroom is on his way to claim his bride and take her back to his home for the marriage feast. The bridesmaids, hearing the groom is coming, possibly from a great distance, go out to wait for him, not precisely sure when he will arrive.

The parable's main point is not that the five foolish girls dozed off to sleep (the wise five also nodded off whilst they waited) but rather that they were unprepared when the summons finally came: "Here is the bridegroom! Come and meet him!" Their foolishness lay in persistent inaction in the face of declining oil reserves. They presumably had as many opportunities as the wise girls to ensure they were ready when the bridegroom arrived. But the difference was, they wasted their opportunities. When at last they woke up to their failure and came to their senses, it was too late.

The setting of this parable in Matthew's Gospel indicates that its message is for disciples (24.3; 26.1), and the context of the parable suggests that its central appeal is to be ready for the climax of God's purposes when Jesus is revealed at the end of time (verse 13, compare with 24.44).

It is a timely appeal for today's Christians and churches, especially in the western world, which is often obsessed with the material and the present to the exclusion of the spiritual and the eternal. This parable draws us on into the future, not to encourage any escapist dreaming, but firstly to remind us that God's good, just and wise plans for his world and his people *will* finally and fully come to pass. In the face of much despair and a mood of meaninglessness and futility, the Christian is marked by a cast iron confidence that history is moving towards a purposeful end, the sign of which will be the coming again of God's Son, Jesus.

Secondly, the parable motivates the disciples of Jesus to get ready for that day. Whether or not it happens in our lifetime, we should be in constant readiness for it. That sense of purpose and hope should therefore shape and determine the choices we make and the priorities we adopt now.

A top athlete, aiming to be the best in his or her chosen event in the next Olympic Games, is highly motivated. That sense of anticipation shapes the many choices which must be made every day: a rigorous training session rather than three hours sitting idly in front of the television, a careful and disciplined diet rather than reckless self-indulgence. And every victory over inaction or a wrong choice furthers the end of being ready when the time of testing arrives.

Life provides for us daily opportunities to prepare for the climax of history. It means choosing those things that build us up and fashion our characters in readiness for the coming of Christ, rather than choosing to live simply for the present and hoping the future will somehow look after itself. The parable brings its searching warning that by our inaction now we can deepen our unpreparedness for that final day of testing.

A further strand of application from the parable is that you cannot borrow another person's accumulated wealth of character. In one sense, when you face life's small or major crises, you stand starkly alone. When you face strong temptations; when you confront difficult problems; when suffering in various forms invades your life; when you at last face the reality of death; how you react at such times will be determined largely by preparations you have made earlier, by the reserves of courage, wisdom, hopefulness and strength which you have allowed God to build into your character before the time of crisis arrives. Such qualities in a person's life are non-transferable; you cannot lend them to or borrow them from another person.

When an elderly Scotsman lay dying, someone offered to read the Scriptures to him. To their surprise he did not seem very eager for this although they knew that all his life he had nourished his heart and his mind on the Bible. They asked him why. His answer was, "Ah theekit ma hoose when the weather was warm". He had thatched his house in the calm weather and now he was ready. He had no need to be ashamed. The times of self-discipline, the right choices made at many moments of decision, when he might have been short-sighted and lived only for the present, had paid dividends and all was well.

IDENTIFYING WITH THE STORY

Recall occasions when you were caught unprepared and you wished you had invested more time in getting ready for the event — perhaps an examination, an occasion when you were entertaining and you had not prepared enough food, an interview for which you had not done your homework. What emotions, such as regret, guilt or frustration, did you feel on those occasions?

QUESTIONS AND ACTIVITIES

1. What dreams and hopes for the short-term and long-term future have your non-Christian friends, relatives and work colleagues? In what ways are they similar to and different from your own?

2. How do you respond to the fact that for two thousand years Christians have expected and longed for the return of Christ, and still it has not happened?

3. If we believe that the only hope for the world is God's final triumph at the coming of Christ, does this mean that we do not need to make the world a better place here and now? Should we just wait eagerly for Christ's return?

4. Think of some specific situations in the coming week when members of the group may be called to make choices, whether small and seemingly insignificant, or major. Talk about how your view of the future

might shape the decisions you make when faced with those choices.

5. At times of crisis there are certain things you cannot borrow. Recall occasions when you have found yourself in some situation of crisis and testing where you realized that no one else could help you. What did you learn from those experiences?

6. In what ways do your church and those linked to it help young people establish good habits and the firm foundations for their lives which will help prepare them for the large and small crises of life?

PRAYER SUGGESTIONS

Give thanks for the assurance that history has a goal, that we have been delivered from the despair about the future, the sense of meaninglessness and futility which fills the lives of many of our contemporaries.

However, while we are in the world we have to cope with ever-changing moods and circumstances which may leave us open to times when we feel negative. Pray for strength, patience and renewed vision to face these times.

Acknowledge before God that so often we choose wrongly when small and major decisions have to be made. Our choices are not shaped by a desire to be ready for Christ's return; we choose rather to spend our energies and resources on things which offer short-term pleasure or satisfaction.

OTHER PASSAGES

Luke 12.35-40
1 Peter 4.7-11
1 John 3.2-3